IMMERSION

ALSO BY MICHELE WOLF

Conversations During Sleep
The Keeper of Light

IMMERSION

POEMS BY

MICHELE WOLF

For Megan,
What a pleasure
to meet you + hear
your work.
Can't wait to
read your book.
Fondly,
Michele

HILARY THAM CAPITAL COLLECTION
SELECTED BY DENISE DUHAMEL

THE WORD WORKS
WASHINGTON, D.C.

ACKNOWLEDGMENTS

My thanks to the editors of the following journals and anthologies, where many of the poems in this collection first appeared:

Confrontation: "Collecting the Wedding Photos," "Why I Became a Journalist"
Crab Orchard Review: "Immersion"
Gargoyle: "Small Talk with an Eight-Year-Old"
Mercy of Tides: Poems for a Beach House (Salt Marsh Pottery Press): "The Great Tsunami"
North American Review: "The Word Fancier"
Poet Lore: "The Midnight Crossing," "Old Mom," "A Street Called Gracie Allen"
Poetry: "The Great Tsunami," "Pocono Lakeside"
Poetry East: "Late Bloomer"
Potomac Review: "Attempting to Fly"
Proposing on the Brooklyn Bridge: Poems About Marriage (Grayson Books): "The Great Tsunami," "Husband-to-Be"
Rattapallax: "Egret"
Rough Places Plain: Poems of the Mountains (Salt Marsh Pottery Press): "Swoon"
Snakebird: Thirty Years of Anhinga Poets (Anhinga Press): "The Great Tsunami," "The Midnight Crossing," "Pocono Lakeside"

Thank you also to the Arts and Humanities Council of Montgomery County, Maryland, for its generous support.

For my two loves,
Sandy and Caroline

Man dies within a hundred years
but is filled with a thousand years of grief.
Since day is short and night seems long
why not wander with a candle
seeking joy while you are in time?
Don't wait for your time to come....

—*Anonymous, first or second century* C.E.,
Han Dynasty, China

CONTENTS

ONE

TWO

ONE

THE GREAT TSUNAMI

She recognizes its crest in the way he looks at her.
The wave is as vast as the roiling mass in the Japanese
Print they had paused in front of at the museum,
Capped with ringlets of foam, all surging sinew.
That little village along the shore would be
Totally lost. There is no escaping this.
The wave is flooding his heart,
And he is sending the flood
Her way. It rushes
Over her.

Can you look at one face
For the whole of a life?

Does the moon peer down
At the tides and hunger for home?

LATE BLOOMER

It flares up at sunrise, a blush in a bramble
Tumbling out of its bed by the city pavement—a single
Rose, coral heat, at the end of the season.
And you are drawn to it, to its scent, its silky
Layers, to its core. It gathers you into its
Body until you lose your balance, all you can see
Is a petaled grid, an endless repetition
Of roses. You sink, swirling, into the rose,
Deep into the rose, into the rose.
I hold you to me. Love, I am forty-four,
And you, love, you, my love,
You have planted me.

IMMERSION

We practice the language, froth of words, that formed
The slosh and current of your life before
You could speak: *"Ni hao ma?"* we greet our teacher,
Who passes out toys and asks us to repeat as she holds up flash cards:
"Panda"—*xiongmao*—followed by "baby," "mother," "father," "dog,"
"Cat." All of the girls in the circle, and the sole boy, are Chinese
Toddlers. Most of the mothers and fathers are middle-aged, white.

At summer's close, we carried you down the blue-tiled steps
Of the synagogue's bath—a swirl of piped-in rainwater,
Municipal water, and a bit of chlorine—and swiftly dipped you
Three times, the water snug to all your surfaces. At the top of the steps
A trio of rabbis chanted the blessings, calligraphied midnight
Blue on the pale blue walls. I recited along in a language I had never
Formally learned, some of the words and all the intonations familiar.

Little flame, you will be the birthright of who you are,
Independent of water or vocabulary.

We work on the words. That's why in the post office, just a few weeks
After we had brought you home, when the Asian American clerk,
In her sixties, spotted you soaking up your new world
From your stroller, puckered up her face, then gazed again at me
And, with accented English, clenching my heart in her hands,
Inquired, "She's yours?" I managed to answer, "Yes. And I'm hers."

Why couldn't she see I had become Chinese?

POCONO LAKESIDE

As I was guided by the director through the thick space
Of these rooms, worn sparrow brown, and strode
With the August sun on my shoulders across this particular
Acre of grass, nobody had told me this was the place
Where you had summered as a boy. I have weathered
My fourth decade, older now than you were
When you died. I can barely remember you, yet I can see
You not as my father but as my son. You are age nine.
The downpour divides into two massive stage curtains
Parting. You bolt from the bunk, loudly racing
With your chums down the slippery hill to the dock,
Your cape of a towel flapping as if ready to lift you airborne.

You are the smallest. Still, you always run in the front.
You do not know how beautiful you are, of course, squinting
Against the sun, the flame that escapes behind the gray
Vapor for hours, sometimes for days. You cannot see
That from the beginning it has been eyeing you from afar,
That it has focused its golden spotlight just for you.

WHY I BECAME A JOURNALIST

I learned early, at age six, while whispering
All the oinks and clucks of "Old MacDonald Had a Farm"
To my father, slumped in his hospital bed, an oxygen
Tube lodged in each of his nostrils—my father tipping
His head to take in my every word—before he died,
Weeks later, at thirty-seven, that we rise for a deadline.

I learned, lost in love with learning, to amass all the facts—
The snowflake decals affixed to the windows as my mother
And I, holding hands, hiked up the five slate flights
Of the hospital's hidden stairs; my father's pallor,
Creamy ocher, like the pages of a grandparent's book
Savored ages before—to learn as much as I could absorb, to adhere
To the space limitations and, using music, get the story out, then
Move on to the next, because there are so many stories to tell.

"Be accurate, be interesting, and be on time," I brought home
From the classroom. Sometimes, as I work at my desk, I almost
Feel a presence behind me, a hand on my shoulder. It is
Not my father. It is my tomorrow. It is the self I will become.

TROPICAL DRINK

It was frothy. It was silken.
It was icy on the tongue—fresh coconut
Milk, fresh pineapple juice, and the Appleton's.
We sipped one apiece on the terrace overlooking
The peaked gazebo cresting the dock, and the glinty
Turquoise waters of our crescent beach, while a big-eyed
Doctor bird—a shimmering long-tailed hummingbird—
Hovered like a miniature copter in front of a blood-red
Hibiscus. When we rocked in the hammock,
The only sound we could hear was the breeze
Fanning the palm fronds. In the pool, on a pair of rafts,
As we closed our eyes in the late-day sun, the whole of our
World turned turquoise, hoisting us, floating us along.
We never drifted far, tethered by the length of your arm,
Of mine, by the buoy of our two hands joined.
And we knew we had tasted the edge of something sweet.

BUS TERMINAL AUBADE

I was new to New York, to the bristling panorama
That is adulthood. New York was old.
Via subway and subterranean walkway, I arrived
At the Port Authority. All I wanted to do
Was get to New Jersey, but at the top of the dingy
Stairs a compact, blue-uniformed security officer
Jabbed a glimmering knife toward the throat of a shaggy,
Staggering man bent into a hook, hunched over
Her, exposed penis erect. The flash of the blade
Emblazoned a flickering corona around the officer.
"Don't you touch me!" she hissed the instant before
She noticed me to her right, then eased her demeanor,
Inching backward. "You can pass, Miss," she offered
Calmly, gesturing with her arm. "You can pass on through."

CHERRY BLOSSOM FESTIVAL

The cloud banks of blossoms—the sudden eruption
Of three thousand century-old trees—surround us at eye level,
Their hint of pink the pigment of plush toys and knitted

Blankets for infant girls. As we stroll the pathway, infused
With this fluff, we just about sprout petals ourselves, embody
Spring as a verb. It was here, in the midst of these blooms, that you

Asked me a question that changed my life, presented a blue
Velveteen box that held up a hard, faceted stone. A woman next to us
Crumpled, in tears. The couple of strangers we approached refused

To stop grinning while taking our pictures: our arms entwined around
Each other, eyes luminous, the backdrop of cherry blossoms
A sheer, lit scrim that fronts what's permanent. What withers, leaves,

Returns, and returns.

RED CLOUD

Surrounded by sentries, the corpus of Mao, draped
In the scarlet national flag, lies placid and waxy
In a crystal casket. Each evening the body
Is lowered into a freezer. Outside Mao's memorial,
Here in Tiananmen Square, the half-mile visitors'
Line, which starts forming at dawn, fans out
From the building. "He is the father of our country,
Just like your George Washington," our soft-spoken guide—
Whose hair is lit with auburn streaks, who studies
American films to master his idioms and his accent—
Informs us, evading our eyes. He was only eleven
Years old at the time of the massacre. A gauze of silence
Seals us. We know what we cannot ask, cannot say.

To our left, at the heavenly gate to the ornate, slope-roofed
Forbidden City, palace complex of the emperors—now
Also home to an art gallery, gift shops, and a Starbucks—
Is a billboard-size portrait of Mao. Fifteen years before,
More than 100,000 protesters, mostly students, camped out
In this square, poured into the avenues, hoisting homemade
Banners, some painted in English: "Strike for Democracy,"
"Strike for Freedom." Hanging from scaffolds, art students
Erected a thirty-foot Statue of Liberty replica, torch held
High, positioned to face this portrait of Mao. Then the tanks
Rolled forward. Assault rifles fired round after round.
Amid the crunch and the screams, the flaming tanks bombed
With Molotov cocktails, blood hung in the air like a fine mist.

ATTEMPTING TO FLY

This was your home. This was the section of town
Where you worked. These were your streets,
Every neglected rut and pothole. These were your
Buildings, damn it, your ATM, your drugstore, deli,
Shoe-repair shop, your Borders Books & Music.
This was your subway station, brace of cars
Screeching along the tracks. These were your neighbors.
You wake up at night, unable to breathe.
These were your neighbors. So when you return
To what was your home, needing to see
Whatever you can see, to walk
The streets, to breathe the air, to breathe
Your neighbors, you expect to find what?
A knuckle hidden under a park bench? A shoelace
Covered with dust? You need to see, and the sign
In front of you, for the workers, reads
"WASH MASK. WASH BOOTS. EAT."

A flatbed truck creeps out to the street with a steel
Girder. The site is concealed from view. You hear
The nonstop pounding and whir of excavation.
A crane pivots. In every direction, abandoned
Buildings are boarded and buttressed. You see
The brightest sky looming, the tallest void.
You see what you saw, as it happened, on TV,
From where you had moved at the end of August,
Two hundred miles from this shrill noise
And absence. You see what you did not see,
What a friend had confirmed from the heights
Of Water Street that morning, what he had witnessed
Again and again, projectile bodies and body parts
Catapulting en masse from the two towers, and those

Still alive, who had elected to leap, who had
Fled being melted down like candle wax,
Flapping their meager wings,
Attempting to fly.

TWO

FIRST KISS

We were sitting on the grass beside the lake's edge
In the dark, a group of us talking, the surface
Marbled by the late-evening light glanced off
Of the moon. Cloaked by the dark,
Caught up with the nearness and the voice
Of this boy from the next town over—handsome
And lanky and smart, shy, with black-lashed
Eyes as jade as a lolling wave before it frays
At the shore—I had no awareness the others had left.

It was a confection, long-lasting and luscious, leaving
Me lost on our private dock. In spite of his promise,
I never heard from him again. Now, thirty years
And three cities later, he enters my living room,
A trauma surgeon interviewed on the TV news. How he
Startles me in his scrubs, still handsome. So he stayed
In Miami. Did he get married? I wonder. Stay married?
Did he father a son who looks the way he did at seventeen?

Across the apartment, my husband sits at his computer,
Preparing a lesson plan. He thinks I am watching an ordinary
Day's chaos on the news. I am watching him—the silhouette
Of his straight back, his impeccable profile. The first night
We kissed, I wore a red balloon butterfly on my head,
A crown I had won playing a game of chance at a Mardi Gras
Carnival. Earlier that evening, after dinner beside the beach,
We had wandered the boardwalk in the dark. As he gathered
Me to him, the roaring ocean seemed to enter all of our
Pores, and soon I would learn he never wanted to let me go.

DESERT SAND

Walter Reed Army Medical Center, Washington, D.C.

The convoy of white buses halts as it meets the green-gowned
Emergency team and double line of white-sheeted gurneys.
The moment the doors fling open, the patients—only two days
Off the field, desert sand caked in their hair, sand streaming
In narrow cascades out of their gear—are whisked into triage,
Beyond the threshold's banner: "We Provide Warrior Care."

This is the polytrauma hospital, for soldiers who return
Ripped apart—war in Iraq, year four. They keep on arriving,
Nearly five thousand since the war began. So many of them live.

Such as the Illinois sergeant whose armor included a sand-colored
Helmet and a mottled vest's mosaic of ceramic plates. His left
Breast pocket held a snapshot—of Christina, age six, his ballerina,
Beside his toddler, Lyle, holding an Elmo doll, and Kelly, his wife,
In her third trimester—when a roadside bomb obliterated his
Humvee, shearing off half of an arm, opaquing his last pinpoint
Of sight. Now, in room 510, on stiff sheets, he settles his nose
In the cove of Kelly's neck. The baby is resting, her heart
Bumping against his chest with the will of a hummingbird, wings
So busy the human eye cannot capture the speed at which they whirl.

WORKING IN THE DISTRICT

Bay after bay, each thick, black outline of a man
Gets pumped with bullets to the heart.
While paying for stamps—with the customers
Behind you queued along a velvet rope,
And a countertop radio, antenna extended,
Purring Beyoncé—you tally the thumps from
The FBI target range that's lodged beneath your feet.

At the base of Pennsylvania, the Capitol glows:
A majestic, squat masked bulb, incandescent.

OLD PATENT OFFICE BUILDING

Walt Whitman Way, Washington, D.C.

The ivory edifice, two city blocks of blasted ridged and pillared
Stone, is an art museum now, a home for presidential portraits.
At winter's edge, March 1865, with the carnage almost over,
Men in tails and women trussed in rustling silk taffeta
Hoop skirts whooped and applauded here as the band sprang
Into "Hail to the Chief" and Lincoln ambled in to greet these
Core believers—four thousand revelers at his second inaugural ball.
This was the evening even Lincoln danced, his wife in his arms.

Just months before, this palace of invention's aisles had housed
A makeshift hospital, where Union soldiers wedged against glass
Cases crammed with toy-size streetcars, looms, accordions,
Tobacco-threshing machines—models of hardened imagination.
"Walt!" "Walt! Hello!" the injured would shout as their friend
Returned. Toting a sack stuffed with oranges and cigars, he
Stopped at the cot of every patient, including the glassy-eyed ones,
Almost gone. For some he read the news, composed a letter.
Or grasped a hand, to blunt the saw being prepped for surgery.

One block north of this broad facade, while attending a comedy,
Our American Cousin, less than a week after Lee—his sword
At his side—had surrendered at Appomattox, Lincoln
Was shot near his left ear and slumped forward. "O Captain!"
The poet pressed on the page, his head too flooded
To lift. And spring continued: flush of azaleas, waft of lilacs.

SMALL TALK WITH AN EIGHT-YEAR-OLD

Mfuwe, Zambia

As I was instructed, I stared in and shook out
My dust-covered shoes every morning, on lookout
For scorpions. That dawn I had stepped forth
From the mosquito netting, the cloud
Surrounding my bed, to discover a spider
The size of my hand in the toilet's pool.
My vista once outside: a welcome of three lumbering
Elephants, shuffling in tandem slow motion along the lagoon.

Now, counting on sunlight, the schoolroom's only light,
I sit among students attentive in cadet-blue uniforms.
None of these children has shoes. The beauty beside me,
Viray, shows me her pages of lessons composed in precise
Block lettering, facts about breast-feeding, why it is
Good. I learn that she helps to take care of her baby
Brother, likes to dance and to cook, that her favorite books
Are the stories of Curious George. A sudden cascade
Of light encases us. The village has no electricity, no
Running water. I learn that at fifteen Viray will marry a man
Whose home includes two other wives, that in this part
Of the world, one of every three adults gets rotted by AIDS.

The previous day, at a private game reserve, I stood
Only inches from the massive yawning jaw of a curious
Lion. Stock-still, I was consumed by its golden eyes,
By the heat of access to those surfaces, two suns. A fence
Protected me. "Do you have to worry about lions at night?"
I asked my new friend, Viray, who lives in a mud cylindrical
Hut that is capped with a thatched roof. Her eyes grew larger.
"Yes!" she answered. "And elephants!" No fences
Anywhere. She would never have believed me
Had I told her that where I live, we must watch out
For lions, too—beware of all the beasts of the earth.

BABY IN A BASKET

This infant was found at the gate of this institute by Miss Li Feng Er and brought in for foster care on 8/29/2003....Our doctor decided her date of birth as 8/26/2003, according to her development. She was named Shang Guan Xu....Shang is the initial of Shanggao [the town]. Guan is the middle name for all kids in this orphanage. Xu means the morning rising sun.
    —*Shanggao Social Welfare Institute Child Development Status Report*

We were ready, with these first photos, for you to be
Cute, but not to be beautiful—which smacked through us
Like a convulsion. We study your startled onyx eyes, alert
As birds at play in a pond, tawny embossed blossom
Of lips, fringe of hair a fluffy nimbus floating above you.

Four months old at the time these were taken, you sit snug
In an oval basket, so overbundled in layers of wool
Sweaters and leggings, you cannot move, your hands
Lost in the soft black tunnels of your vast jacket's sleeves.
Our agency suggests we tell you a story from long before
You can understand: In China your Birth Mommy—who had
Held you curled inside her for nine months—and Birth Daddy
Loved you very much, but could not keep you, so they made
A plan. They wrapped you in blankets, set you in a basket,
And delivered you someplace safe, where they knew
Kind people would care for you until your
Forever Mommy and Daddy could take you home.

For now you sit, as the hours pass, in a worn metal
Crib, in a room wall-to-wall with cribs, each shared by two
Burbling girls, and here in our hands, propped up
In a basket, waiting for the slow, slumbering
World to turn your way. You are our morning rising sun.

OLD MOM

For my daughter

As I wheel you and our purchases—toothpaste, Similac—toward
A register, our cashier murmurs to a colleague in a language
She thinks I don't understand: *"La abuela,"* she says with certainty.

I am certain I will not be alive the day you turn forty.
You have just learned how to walk. Your unscuffed sneakers,
Glossy white with fuchsia stripes, crisp knotted laces flecked

With silver, flash hot-pink lights with each new step, as bright
As the sunshine in your face when you shuffle toward me—arms
Raised, holding your palms forward for balance—still amazed

You can locomote yourself with two extremities only, and alone.
And when I am indeed old, once you have clocked the hurdles
Of thirty and thirty-five, with more years ahead of you

Than behind, please also see me as I was that summer and fall
Once we brought you home, the way I would carry you,
A scrawny toddler who couldn't toddle, couldn't crawl,

Couldn't grasp and deliver to her mouth a morsel of bread,
Ate like a just-hatched wren, from the palm of my hand.
Sitting on the rug, we'd practice a game with the slats

Of your playpen—your laugh a swift clinking of bells—
As I would encourage you "Up, up, up," demonstrating a way
For you to lift yourself, hand over hand. Soon you were scooting

Along the furniture, then reaching for my index fingers,
Marching ahead with one in each hand, until you discovered,
With me by your side, you could walk on your own.

ACCIDENT

The white-masked doctor, swathed by the fierce
Light from the white globe at the ceiling,
Slid off my scalpeled, blood-soaked panties,
High in the light with my lifted
Ankles, the droopy leg holes a pair
Of punctures in a strange, deflated balloon,
Once blue. We were not playing rough,
Only hide-and-seek, when I bashed
Through a glass door so clear
I thought it was open. I lay
In a puddle of blood, glass chunks
And thin, pointy splinters raining upon me.
Now I sit still like a good girl, bandaged
From hip to ankle, sixty stitches in my left
Thigh alone. My whole leg is a numb lump—
I can't wiggle my toes, not even my
Big one. My aunt hugged me, kissed me,
Promised to return with my mother
At three-thirty. I miss my cousins.
I'm bored with these quiet games—coloring
Books, connect the dots, Colorforms, puppets,
Puzzles. Whenever the nice nurse
Passes, I ask the time. She straps her watch
To my wrist, tapes it in place with a Band-Aid.
The second hand sails round and round,
But the others are so slow. I do not know
That the doctors say I may never
Walk again, that my mother, two hundred
Miles away, slammed down the receiver, ran
Screaming to the bedroom to pummel
The pillow, gagging over and over, "No! No! No!"
That my father, shriveled by a third,
His skin the color of mustard, wincing

And weak on a different hospital bed,
Will be dead in eight months. I only know
That at twenty minutes after three,
Dark-haired and delicate, the essential
Princess from the storybook I have learned
Best, she arrives—the most beautiful
Woman in the world, all sad eyes
And bright smile. I bounce on the bed
As she rushes to greet me. Everything
Will be fine now. She is
The love of my life,
Mommy.

THE MAGIC KINGDOM

At the end of each stick arm is a white-gloved sphere:
A clutch of four chubby fingers plus a cushiony
Palm. Mickey has yet to install his craniofacial
Dome atop his neck. "Princess Castle!" my daughter
Shouts as soon as she spots the spired, mock-stone
Facade, blue turrets shining. (You can't go inside,
Check out Cinderella's shoe carousel, for instance.)
It's almost showtime—parents are busy positioning
Key essentials: children, camcorders, cameras.
I lodge my girl on the shelf of my hip. She stares
Transfixed, the apertures of her eyes and mouth

Fully open, as Mickey and cronies—Minnie, Donald,
Goofy, and a trio of tiaraed princesses, dotingly escorted
By their princes—dance and cavort onstage until, in a blast
Of smoke, the black-draped Evil Fairy arrives, pledging
Nightmares for all. My daughter, pressing her head
To my neck, confesses, "I don't like that bad witch,
Mommy." She'll disappear, Mickey tells us, if the whole
Crowd concentrates and shouts, "Dreams come true!"—
Which thunders out of me and the child I am holding.
We repeat this over and over. The polished land
We are visiting is canned, yet there is a knot
In my throat. And two brackish canals, carrying me
On the gondola ride to my future, line my cheeks.

CHINESE NEW YEAR, USA

You sit on your father's shoulders, compact work
Of art that you are, dressed in your scarlet
Suit with mandarin collar, flower-bud closures
On the diagonal, silk brocade embroidered with metallic
Gold bouquets on pants and top. The crackling red,
Fierce bonfires of joy and radiance, glows throughout the room—
On fat globed lanterns, banners hung from the ceiling, envelopes stuffed
With candy or cash, the gaping jaw of the sixty-foot gold-scaled
Dragon, paraded on poles by dancers snaking across the stage.
At only two, you already clap on cue with the crowd.

Strolling up to you with a high five is your father's giggly, straight-A
Student Courtney Kuo, who had confided she likes french fries way
Better than rice—somehow she always burns rice—and that the kids
Whose parents arrived in the States from China or Taiwan
Don't really accept her, keep to themselves. She wears a fuzzy pink
Turtleneck, a pink and cerise chenille scarf, pink flat suede boots,
A pink phone, and acid-washed low-rider jeans (belly button concealed).

With the thrust of a bamboo "sword," the martial arts solos begin.
You sit on the pedestal of your father's shoulders, cheering
Each practiced kick. Your original parents will never be known.
Now you live in a land of plenty, where someday you can
Learn to speak Italian if you wish, *bellissima,* pilot a plane,
Rise like a lotus blossom, reaching for the heavens, all perfume.

THREE

THE MIDNIGHT CROSSING

Your mother had stepped away from the table, and so
Had you. I sat facing your father. Though neither
Would say so, both of us knew something was wrong.
He brought up an article I had written, about ways
For couples to approach fighting fairly, about getting
Along. He had been married close to fifty years. "Don't
Say everything on your mind," he told me. "That works."

On the night of your father's funeral, we drift into sleep,
Two nested question marks, realizing, in our middle
Years, how little life has prepared us for. When we shift
In the night, your hands reach over to find mine, each
Seeking its interlocking mate. By day, on a deadline,
You rewrite computer code. In your field, this millennial
New Year, the double-aught New Year, is known as
The midnight crossing. With midnight's arrival, you
Will discover whether you have missed something critical.

Your father believed in love and in logic, not in God or
An afterlife. Yet, no good at disappearing, he visits
In dreams. "Dad, what are you doing here?" you ask him,
Astonished. "You're dead." "Oh, no," he explains to you.
"I have eleven more days." "Really?" you say. "That's great!
We'll do something. We'll make the most of it." Then,
With a casual wave, your father, smiling, steps out the door.

SWOON

You had a pink nose, all stuffed up,
And couldn't breathe. Our arms linked,
We made our way back to my apartment.

It was good-night time, late, the last moments
Of our second date. In a flash, you lifted me
A full foot above you and kissed me smack at the spot

Where my heart beats, at the hint of my cleavage.
I thought I would swoon. I wanted to remain
There, aerial, never needing the ground,

Aloft in your arms, your sweet lips pressed
Against my skin, like clouds to a highland.

EATING MINNOWS

He had assumed he was eating french fries
Until he realized each of the short, golden
Sticks bore eyes. As he chewed, he pictured
The swimmers, a shimmery ghost-gray,
Careening among weeds
Of a lake bottom, boggy, considered
The crunch of the fries, plus
The task of bait impaled on a hook,
Cast out, the art of disguise.
He remembered the taste
Of being lured by distant eyes.

EGRET

You always stand alone, silent, along the cattails,
Beside the edge of the pond, your elegant stalk
Of a neck—stark, sinuous, elongated *S*—
Pale pineapple sleek beak, so poised in repose,
Almost motionless, for hours. The others—
The ibises, ambling the grounds like a convocation
Of squat storks; the squawking geese, blasting
At each passing human, anticipating food;
The placid ducks, nestling plump on a neighbor's
Lawn, as if incubating their young—always
Travel in flocks. You are ever alone, giraffe
Of the bird world, requiring no one, self-contained.

Yet wait: As the sky turns slate, you extend
Your neck, a supple pointer stretched to the hilt,
Out toward the horizon. Again, you look locked
In place. What are you listening for so intently,
Now flooded with yearning? In clusters of waves,
The dark, roiling clouds roll east. They are
Not threatening. No, they are only doing their job.

COUSINS' CLUB REUNION

As we hug hello on the whitewashed porch
Or form thickets of lawn chairs beside
The shade trees, I always count on
The dozens of lost names to flit back to me.
Most of them do, each of these last links
To my father—beloved "crown prince of the family,"
My sole surviving great-aunt, about to turn ninety-two,
Shaking the crook of her pointer finger, calls him—
Consumed young by the slow acid of cancer, winter
1961. Each of my father's cousins always knows me.

I always learn something. "Did you know
That once in the forties in Florida, a bus driver
Ordered your father, whose tan was really deep,
To move to the back?" one relative tells me.
A family member I do not recognize approaches.
Though it is mid-July, he is hidden in a sweatshirt,
Extends his hand in a white knitted glove. The shade
Of his face is an off-cerise, an opaque purple-red rose.
"Michele," he says, "I'm Joel. How are you?"—a voice
I recognize. He is not a human color, yet here he stands.

He has come to the Cousins' Club. As the day escapes,
He sits at the base of a shade tree, a gloved hand
Cupping the hand of his elder daughter against
His chest. She stands behind him and over him, a tall
Canopy of shade herself. His cousins' voices—a chirpy,
Reverberant buzz—surround him. It does not matter
What anyone says. The tufts of lawn beneath his feet,
Springy and crisp, are grasshopper green, and the bower
Of sky that towers above him, an ashy splash that rides
The horizon, eases into a balmy, swimming pool blue.

For Joel Horvitz, 1943–2006

BARBIE SLITS OPEN HER DIRECT-MAIL OFFER TO JOIN AARP

My worth is most inflated when, on tiptoes, I pose
In my original box, never handled, especially if I date
Back to '59 or '60. But that is rare. I am more used
To breaking out, to being the damp flamingo
Pecking to leave the shell. I prefer moving forward.
I was an astronaut in '65, a surgeon in '73. Last year
Was golden, a field of sunflowers waving in the wind:
I earned $1.2 billion and, through my foundation,
Funded a state-of-the-art children's hospital.
I never had children, although I certainly
Schtupped my brains out. "Excuse me," you say,
"You don't have a vagina, or any internal organs."
That's where you are wrong—so entranced
By my smooth casing that you do not recognize
What a doll is. I am a metaphor. I am
My owner's vessel for dreams. I can be almost
Anything: warrior, soothsayer, princess. Imagination
Starts as soft clay but becomes a polished thing.
In this sense, yes—with the occasional big-eyed Dora or
Velveteen, croaky SpongeBob—I have been a parent.

It's the "almost" that still weighs on me at times. And
You should know that the surgeries have been painful.

I used to be young.

THE CARAPACE

Skin, although she did remember its give,
Was an impossibility. She could still
See the tip of the stranger's knife, positioned
To dig a pit near her nostril, and the gaze
Of her ghost, frozen, that lost face
Pinned to the wall of glass, watching
The stranger fist his knife up between
Her legs, through membrane and womb
And belly, fisting it, smooth fin, through
The waters to her heart, to the edge of her
Soul pouch. "Not that," she mouthed.
The sound crouched, refusing to come out.
And then he carved, until a stillness
Bled through her and time went black.

Her flesh turned to mineral, a plated carapace,
Numb to the touch. Slowed to a sleepwalk,
A primitive muscle memory, she considered
Herself an abstraction—her body, a prop.
She allowed no one near. Keeping watch
At her dead place, she tested her pulse points
Morning and evening—wrists, temples,
Neck—until, the extent of another girlhood
Later, a quake jolted her chest and the carapace
Pinched her, as tight as a tourniquet, until it
Cracked into shards at her feet, revealing
A sheath of silky fresh skin, as damp as
The curve of an eye, unaccustomed to light.

On a low shelf, beside a photo of her younger self,
Is a chip of the carapace. She sets it on her palm
With a mother's love for a child evicted

Out of her skin, a singular child who believed
She was so intelligent, so clever with words,
Who assumed that a proper arrangement
Of sounds was her shield and her armor.

THE GRIEVING ROOM

I.
Your eyes are open, blank, fixed.
They are not like the eyes of the sleeping,
Lids a hairbreadth lifted, eyes calm
Or, in the trance of a dream, fluttering.
Nor like the eyes stilled in a photograph,
Flat but familiar,
Reliable glimpses into a soul.
Nor even like two glossy stones
At the foot of a pond,
One moment clear and then,
When the wind
Rumples the surface, far away.
They are eyes of the dead.
Pressed to the bed rail, we stand
Over you, a mother flanked
By two daughters only, arm in arm,
Watching you heave
With each blast of the ventilator.
Your heart repeats
Its jagged scrawl across the screen.
You are already there,
At your destination,
Already worlds beyond our sky.
What do you see, my sweet Cathy,
What do you see?

II.
I cannot bring myself
To touch your cheek, to kiss you,
Take your hand,
This body
That was once my sister.
Later you would show me
Where you had journeyed,
Through shadows to a circle
Of loved ones, floating in a grotto
With soft walls of burgundy-gray cloud.
Each face shone with replenished youth.
Our grandmother Rose, not as she died
But dark haired, in her bloom at forty,
Rocked you against her,
As did the others in turn, overcome
By that silent crying
In which the chest swells
But the eyes no longer tear.
In spite of your weariness
You reached toward those first
Welcoming arms, the arms
Of our father, who also arrived
Here young, before you began to speak.
And yet how you recognized him,
How you did know him.

III.
In line at the hospital cafeteria
I chose chicken soup for our mother,
Turkey and mashed potatoes for me.
It was the longest wait,
Once your brain had died,
For your sturdy heart to follow.
The room was draped in tinsel and snowflakes.
The speakers were caroling "Deck the Halls."
"Have some cake, dear," offered the serving
Woman. "As much cake as you'd like.
Merry Christmas!"
"Thank you," my voice answered dully,
A reflex. "Merry Christmas to you."
How much I resembled
That life-size mechanical Santa
At the entrance, his slow-motion waving—
The way I chewed, then attempted
To swallow, turkey,
Each bite lodged in my throat,
The way I roused myself this morning
To dress for a funeral.
That was how we spent December 25,
The day on which our present
Was not given, but taken away.
A present we were permitted to borrow,
But too exquisite to keep,
Wrapped in roses,
Scattered with earth.
And one last time,
Before you are lowered,
I touch your polished wooden box.

IV. *For our mother*
I sleep to the side in her oversize bed.
When she cries in the night,
I offer my hand,
But even I am unable to reach her.
"Her life was so sad," she blurted out
This morning, eyes filling again,
Reminded of surgeries, tantrums,
Breakdowns—how you never quite fit in.
And in the grocery store or a restaurant
Every voice she hears, the back
Of each young woman's head,
Seems to be yours.
Your kitchen chair
Since you sat on a phone book
To reach the table
Remains cavernous, empty.
She keeps expecting you to return,
Singing one of those sugary
Hit songs as you set out the plates,
Brimming over with news of your students—
How Jasmine no longer reverses her *R*'s
And Adam can write his first name.
Dozens of visitors stop by the house,
Yet no one can comfort her.
She sits on a stiff chair
Tucked in a chamber inside her heart
Where no one can enter.
The curtains are drawn.
It is stuffy with a heavy
Shifting darkness, a room
Full of shadows. She is
Wailing, beseeching,
Quavering, her arms
Uplifted, fingers splayed,
Reaching at shadows.

For Cathy Wolf, 1958–1982

AFTER ROUGH SEAS

I am still rocking, still on the boat, although my feet
Have known land for days. The foundation
Of sea swaggers beneath me as if these streets—thick
With pillars of concrete and pockets of plush
Green—were just a stiff tarp on the deep. I am
Still on the boat, being tossed by the Mediterranean
At midnight, being ricocheted pinball-style, bouncing
Left right left, from banister to banister, all the way
Down the hall. For some on the cruise, the constant seesaw
Of the sea was too severe. The unseen crew had placed
A pair of empty takeout-food containers, flaps
Raised—a corps of flame-free luminarias, two ivory
Strands lighting my path—in front of each door.

Now back home, I rock, pause at the curb as horns honk.
As soon as the light changes, I walk, hauling my bags,
Balanced, as ballast. Staring ahead, as I fix on the fluttering
Litter stuck to the gutter's grates, I walk a straight line.

COLLECTING THE WEDDING PHOTOS

It was more than the quality of the light or a trick
Of the filter. Our four hundred proofs had neglected
To note the passage of time, as if, for one pivotal
Day, our faces had shone with only the future,
Spared of the roads of all the places we had been.

"This is it, hon. Turn here," I told my new husband
As we followed the map of this unfamiliar island, choosing
A detour because, weeks earlier, our wedding photographer
Had moved. We had just stashed our ivory faux-leather
Albums, nestled in tissue and boxed, in the trunk.

Turning, we entered the gate to the green swath promised
By the map. On our wedding day, under the canopy,
Turning from the rabbi to my husband-to-be, all I could see was
My husband—not who else was there, not who was not there.
All I could see was the measure of light in my husband's eyes.

Beyond the gate was the field of stones, home to my father,
Lowered forty years before. The office was silent, closed.
I stood next to my husband facing the thousands of stones, each
Hosting its own surface of grass, each blade awake in the jostling
Wind. I struggled to recall a picture buried long ago.

"We'll find him," my husband said, and so we roamed.
For an hour we drove the pathways, reading as many names
As we could, never locating the gray marker we needed:
Block 38, Row 17, Grave 2. Soon after, I would call to ask
The hours on a holy day. "The gate is always open," I was told.

FOUR

A STREET CALLED GRACIE ALLEN

Because we were numb, because all our muscles had lumbered,
Weighted, throughout the day, your brother and I
Loaded our hearts into our suitcase along with our funeral suits.
The evening before, content with your Friday-special takeout—
The still-warm veal Milanese, poached asparagus, a Coke—
You had been ambling back toward your parked car
In the dark, crossing Wilshire, when the Mercedes, black
As the pupils of your eyes, rammed into you, finally stopped.

We enter the hospital every morning on a street called Gracie Allen.
"Wake up, Garrett," I plead in my own skull, shouting above
The repeating singsong bleat of the monitors, the whoosh
Of the ventilator. The coma nurse tells us you will not remember
How to brush your teeth, the way to guide a fork up to your
Mouth. We wait by your side. Each day, as if manufactured,
The climate is sunny and crisp. Across from our hotel, a billboard
Marked "Fetish" sports a tawny model with marcelled platinum
Hair, stiletto thigh-high boots, a scrap of skirt skimming
Her thighs. She is surrounded by a latticed lacing of barbed wire.

Every town, tiny or large, has its character. The last time we visited,
We clicked a picture of me with my palms in Marilyn's prints.
This time the Terminator is omnipresent on TV, running
For governor. Yackety women in halter tops anchor the news.
We know it's absurd, yet what we yearn for is a black-and-white
Hollywood ending: You open your eyes in a haze, grimace,
Then crack some jokes, bound out of bed. But when the doctors
Banish us for twenty-four hours, we descend with no bottom,
Until we enter the ICU and your A.M. nurse effervesces,
"He's talking!" We tiptoe inside, and now we are the ones
Who cannot breathe, astounded to see you sitting up, your green
Eyes lively. "Come over here and let me kiss you," you say to your mom
As we greet the day, in this city of flames, city of roses, city of angels.

TWO FIELDS

The Conservatory Garden, Central Park

He had zoomed a menu right up to his face, and still
Couldn't read it. Yet he resisted giving in
To a new prescription, to two disparate fields.
With special lenses, only he would know, but it pained
Him to think of receiving the world by way of a split
Screen, an ongoing battle between distance and close by.

They settle on a bench on the stone balcony overlooking
The green, groomed smooth, a ripened meadow
Flanked by banks of billowing crabapple trees.
The wedding party below them pauses, then, in parade, trails
Its tuxedoed photographer to the flower gardens—irises,
Honeysuckle, roses—a lovely fuss removed by
A crabapple wall from the peace of this plush patch.

She looks at him, so disappointed with the world, with what
He expected his life to be like, and what has withdrawn
From view. The eyes change—they were art-directed
That way—and creases subtly etch the skin
Around them. How much, though, the eyes
Appear the same, with the same longing and spark.
In spring, giddy, flush with the heat, the knobby,
Stark wisteria arbor becomes an umbrella of purple
Blossoms. Crabapples erupt with their pink froth.

MIGRATION OF SAND

Forlorn as a shipwreck, the hulking invader sits
Moored at the shoreline, wheezing
And spewing the dredge ferry's crystalline
Cargo, vacuumed from a distant quarry
On the ocean floor. How it mars the view,
This shuttling and dumping to stave off
The ocean. Not that you assumed
You would find, unsullied, the beach
Of your childhood—the worn, gritty picnic
Tables, stationed in pairs near the parking lot,
Under the palms, or the clumpy filigree
Of seaweed at water's edge, hemming in
The morning's jackpot mounds
Of seashells, pounded smooth. Now,
As the water ruffles against your calves
And a flurry of gulls lingers, transformed
Into sentries manning the shore,
Even the shifting sea seems unfamiliar.

You squint at the sun—hard, blistering
Anchor. For years you dozed
On this beach's sand, a pillowy mattress
That conformed to all your contours—
Until you fled, rarely able to hold still,
Much less notice the drift. The beach
Refeeding, you would later learn, would be
A huge success, avoiding harm to turtles,
Coral reefs, and the hard bottom of the sea.
It is possible, engineers would prove,
To reclaim paradise, to clear
The walls that cinch time,
To resurrect a disappearing way of life.

ARRANGING THE BOOKS

The shelves start out with Ai, move on to the coral
Spine of Miss Bishop. In my new home, in a new city, I rip
Open my next carton and stop. I have somehow misplaced
Mr. Merwin before Mr. Merrill, which has to be fixed.

I am again at Scribner's, a bastion—with its Beaux Arts bookstore,
Frilled with curly cast iron and gilt—at this site on Fifth since
Engines edged out hoofbeats on the avenue. I had just been
Promoted from editorial assistant to associate editor. The rooms
Displayed the relics of their ghosts: a bust of Hemingway,
The lectern of Max Perkins—who elected to stand, as if addressing
His authors, to edit. The wood-walled library featured fringed
Lampshades; reception, a scuffed and tack-studded tobacco-brown
Leather couch. Young Charlie, newly ensconced in the coveted
Corner Perkins office, brought in a piano, serenaded Scottie
Fitzgerald as my colleagues and I rolled our eyes, pretended to work.

Soon Atheneum arrived, a doomed move to keep the two companies
Private. On weeknights I raced off to readings, attempted to write,
Paged through my textbooks—stacks of jacketed works by Atheneum
Poets: the pedestaled Justice, Levine, Merrill, Merwin, and Strand.

Now, two and some decades later, I have divorced New York.
My soul mate, it understands and forgives me. We are on
Friendly terms. I did not get to cart off the Metropolitan Museum
When I left, or the halting schools of yellow cabs, or the window
Booth at the local diner, or the all-night neon of 86th Street,
But I did get to take the books, to keep their voices, vital, intact.
I have Mr. Merrill, diminutive, regal at the podium, infinitely
Wry, regaling the audience—gasping with laughter—with a vision
Of an uncapped lipstick and a randy, panting Labrador, 1935.
I have Mr. Merwin, rumpled, just in from Hawaii, surrounded

By five writers summoned to a table at the 92nd Street Y,
Focused on his eyes, a crystal blue like captured starlight,
On the crux of his message, the sound and essence of his life:
"We don't write poems," he maintained. "We listen for them."

THE WORD FANCIER

It began with a dabbling in stories,
Until the getting from here to there
Lost its allure. Then the pleasures
Of poetry, one word
Easing up to its neighbor,
The two joining hands, swooping
Out the door. Until the lines
Became reduced to discrete
Units—then further to syllables,
Phonemes, digraphs, to dignified
Vowels like a tenor's notes—units
Of meaning and sound and mystery,
Entire dominions unto themselves.
Much as a jeweler appraises an emerald
Or a biologist harvests a cell,
This was her calling, to observe
Language, to pare down its layers
To get to its pulse, lost in the depths
Of the eddies, the spell,
Of *Iridescence,*
Rhododendron,
Ocarina.

HUSBAND-TO-BE

We are on the phone in distant cities, and you are trying
To find the words. I think you might cry.

How about: "It was sudden. One day when I looked
At your face, I looked in my own eyes."

How about: "When your body surrounds me, I know
I have finally arrived in the landscape of my home,
A refuge I have wandered decades to find."

How about: "My heart is a sandpiper, flying over
The waves as it heads to a warmer shore,
Informed by the ocean's roar that land is near."

Any words, or an absence of words,
Will serve. I love you, too.

SKIN

I was peeling a tangerine for you, pulling apart
The webbed, juicy lobes, digging out
The occasional seed, when you—too young
To recognize any boundaries between us—sprang,
As if winged, into my lap and, nose to nose
With me, mirrored my gaze. "Mommy,"
You squealed, cupping my cheeks
With your hands, "I have a yellow face!"
How thin skin is. "Who would say such a thing
To a baby?" I raged to myself in the next
Split second. But before I could say, "Honey,
You are golden" and "All skin colors are
Beautiful," you announced, "I'm a bumblebee!"—
Then flitted away to your garden of toys,
The whir of the world hurtling past flesh
To send sparks through your mind's gray furls.

BALANCED ROCK

Arches National Park, Utah

Never teetering, it has held tight to its craggy base for millennia:
This red-orange sandstone worn away by water and wind.
It angles forward into the massive sky, the padded fence
That marks the divide between us and oblivion.
We see only sky, with its scattered gauze of clouds,
And miles of red-orange rubble interrupted by monoliths.
Joining us in the August heat are fellow pilgrims here to admire
The slabs and arches and fins. I stand with your father, who,
After years by my side, I sometimes forget is not myself
And watch as you march ahead of us on the path, so eager
To lead the way, a child who supplies her own sun and garden
Wherever she goes. Today, in a coral and lemon floral
Sundress, you stare at the rock and ask, "Why doesn't it fall?"

And your weathered parents, contoured by a smash of glass
Piercing the flesh, by the glint of a captor's knife, fixed
Into a glossy, pearlized handle, by the early fade
And death of two reliable rocks of fathers, by the blood
On the brain of a broken sister claimed young—your two
Parents, on vacation, giddy with a sense of well-being
And light, lift you while we laze on the cliff top
We travel every day, parents ever mindful of what we have.

DAUGHTER

It was my dream that you grow up with your new parents beside the bay in San Francisco, America—far from the dust of China, yet surrounded by an ongoing cascade of Chinese voices, by your reflection facing you in Chinese eyes.

True, you could be an exotic bird in Spain or Ireland or Norway—Norway!—but most of the women who crave daughters and cross the world to get to China—women with wombs still vacant in spite of so many years of trying, so much seed—arrive from America, where the state doesn't dictate how many children you may have. Where education, set before you like a twelve-course banquet at a wedding, is free until university. Where a person isn't disparaged as "peasant" for wilting labor in the fields. Where any child who studies hard is offered the privilege of university—this is heaven, yes?—to cultivate her own gifts and honor her own self.

I knew, well before the nausea set in, that I couldn't keep you, as much as I wanted you. When my period never arrived and I soon discovered the faint stain and the plastic IUD—its copper bands as shiny as a piece of jewelry—in my underwear, I knew what I had to do. Each second was critical. Just weeks before, at the family-planning station, white-coated Mrs. Huang had confirmed that my required IUD—the only birth control you can get in this town, aside from sterilization—was in place. In seven weeks I was scheduled to have my next IUD check. The family-planning committee requires an inspection every three months.

For China to thrive, it has to restrict its population. But for years the people have been haunted by the miserable IUDs, always failing, and by the quotas, not only for every family but for the entire town. The family-planning cadres get bonuses, of course, for enforcement. Couples who have a boy are not allowed to have an additional child. In some places couples who have a girl are permitted to try again for a boy—parents rely on a son to support them when they're old—and must pay an impossible sum, three times their annual pay, if they have that child.

For these families, two children is the limit. Everyone has heard of the poison syringe. Thugs kidnapped Li Juan, of Linyi, *two days* before she was due and pinned her down on a clinic table, where a monster shoved a needle deep into her belly. Her baby girl was born dead, then dunked in a water bucket, just to be sure.

I couldn't end you. So I didn't tell anyone about you, not even your father, because I knew he would be practical. "What choice do we have?" he'd say. Even if we could somehow hide the pregnancy and have you, we'd lose our jobs. We've heard rumors about homes being hacked with sledgehammers. But I had a plan. I would get a job at the tannery in Yichun, in Jiangxi Province, where my cousin works as a supervisor and his wife's uncle is manager. I would send money home to my precious Wei Shan—your big brother, my chess champion and climber, always sitting in a tree—your father, and his parents, knowing I wouldn't be able to see them and my parents and sisters again until after the birth. I would leave before the pomegranates bloomed and return before they ripened. I would live with my cousin's family. I would have you.

When I left for Yichun with my residence permit, I was almost three months pregnant. Your father, oddly, never figured it out, but the evening I arrived, my cousin's wife, who knew there had to be a reason for the immediacy, looked me in the eyes and clutched my shoulders. "What will you do?!" she asked, terrified. "What will you do?!" I told her my plan.

I brought my fake-name, forged birth permit to the local family-planning station and told the cadre I was delighted, of course, to be expecting my first child, whom my mother-in-law would be raising in Shandong Province. All along I had the sense you were a girl, but I didn't know for sure until I'd had my first sonogram. "China needs its lovely flowers, its little girls," I said in earnest to the doctor. She paused, no longer permitted to reveal the gender—so many more girls than boys have been aborted over the years. She stared at me, this doctor who had to perform every obstetric procedure, this doctor who had become old young. She finally answered, "You will be a most fine, warm-hearted mother." So I knew.

I worked a nine-hour day cutting shoe leather, until my water broke. You surged out of me after just over an hour of contractions, your perfect tiny hands balled into fists. How I held you, precious girl, watched your chest rise and fall while you slept, fed you from my breasts when you awoke crying. I clipped your hair, which I keep in a small red satin case. I never named you. This was the plan: for you to have the best life possible, a life in America. On the third day, in the opaque night, when my cousin and his wife said it was time, I howled as if my lungs were being clawed out of my chest. Although it was August, I wrapped you in two layers of pajamas and three blankets, set you in a basket, and gave you to my cousin to take in the borrowed car to the Shanggao orphanage, several towns away. He parked far from the pebbled driveway and walked to the gatehouse that greets visitors before the entrance, the gatehouse lit with perpetual light, where we knew someone would discover you once the sun's flames woke the sky at dawn.

女儿

Daughter, I entrust you to your new American parents, who adore you. Your American mother—to whom I'm indebted, but whose imagination is richer than moon cakes—made up my story. She did not, however, conjure the sorrow of Li Juan, who is real. No, you'll never find me, not in the way you wish, not even once you return to the dust and bad air of China. Yet know that I loved you and that I continue to love you every time I draw breath. I gave you your life. I'm with you always. Simply look at your own face. I live in your eyes. I live in the wind that rustles the branches and leaves of the trees wherever you walk, that lifts your hair and swiftly drapes it across your cheek. I am your spirit.

ARCHAEOLOGY

The storm had bitten away the shoreline,
Leaving behind a whiskered nine-foot cliff,
And underneath it the hard-packed sand
Was littered with starfish. Jutting
Out of the cliff bottom, stripped
Free of its tomb at water's edge,
Was the back third of a tan
Metallic 1952 Buick, license lost.
No cars, aside from jeeps, were allowed
On the island. The ocean darted
Forward and back, inspecting its find.

This morning the splintering ribs
Of the hull of an eighteenth-century ship
Arose in the spongy crater of mud
At the site of the World Trade Center,
Twenty feet below street level. Artifacts
Are the accounts we leave behind.
We leave them buried beneath what is buried,

Much as we live in our beauty now.
We may expose only the husk of ourselves,
But embedded and patient in our subterranean
Core, removed from use for so long that most
Have become forgotten, are every memory,
Every gesture, every meandering
Thought. And that's just the library. Jammed
Into the great room—some wearing boots,
Some barefoot—our ancestors are dancing.
We can feel them in our bones.
They're stomping the floorboards.

NOTE: The story of Li Juan, described in "Daughter," is from an account in *Time*, September 12, 2005.

ABOUT THE AUTHOR

Michele Wolf is the author of *Conversations During Sleep*, winner of the Anhinga Prize for Poetry, and *The Keeper of Light*, selected for the *Painted Bride Quarterly* Poetry Chapbook Series. Her poems have appeared in *Poetry, The Hudson Review, Boulevard, North American Review*, and many other literary journals and anthologies. A contributing editor for *Poet Lore*, she has received an Anna Davidson Rosenberg Award and fellowships from Yaddo, the Edward F. Albee Foundation, the Virginia Center for the Creative Arts, the Helene Wurlitzer Foundation of New Mexico, and the Arts and Humanities Council of Montgomery County, Maryland. She has also been a Scholar in Poetry and served on the administrative staff at the Bread Loaf Writers' Conference. Raised in Florida and a longtime New Yorker, she now lives with her husband and daughter near Washington, D.C., where she works as an editor and teaches at The Writer's Center.

ABOUT THE COVER ARTIST

Atlanta artist Hellenne Vermillion creates oil paintings influenced by her life in Japan, where she grew up. She received a BFA in Ceramics from Georgia State University. Vermillion combines the sense of calm and serenity felt in the temples of Japan with the openness and colorful aspects of American life. Her paintings depict flow and movement through space. She also works with silk dye painting and clay sculpture and teaches in the Atlanta area.

ABOUT THE HILARY THAM CAPITAL COLLECTION

The Hilary Tham Capital Collection (HTCC) is an imprint of The Word
Works featuring juried selections from poets who volunteer to assist The
Word Works in its mission to promote contemporary poetry. Judge Denise
Duhamel selected the HTCC books for 2011.

Hilary Tham was the first author published in the Capital Collection
imprint, in 1989. In 1994, when she became Word Works Editor-in-Chief, she
revitalized the imprint. At the time of her death in 2005, Ms. Tham had paved
the way for publication of thirteen additional Capital Collection titles. The
series, renamed in her honor, continues to grow.

THE HILARY THAM CAPITAL COLLECTION

Mel Belin, *Flesh That Was Chrysalis*, 1999
Doris Brody, *Judging the Distance,* 2001
Sarah Browning, *Whiskey in the Garden of Eden,* 2007, 2nd printing 2011
Grace Cavalieri, *Pinecrest Rest Haven*, 1998
Christopher Conlon, *Gilbert and Garbo in Love,* 2003
   Mary Falls: Requiem for Mrs. Surratt, 2007
Donna Denizé, *Broken Like Job*, 2005
W. Perry Epes, *Nothing Happened*, 2010
James Hopkins, *Eight Pale Women*, 2003
Brandon Johnson, *Love's Skin*, 2006
Judith McCombs, *The Habit of Fire*, 2005
James McEwen, *Snake Country*, 1990
Miles David Moore, *The Bears of Paris*, 1995
   Rollercoaster, 2004
Kathi Morrison-Taylor, *By the Nest*, 2009
Michael Schaffner, *The Good Opinion of Squirrels*, 1996
Maria Terrone, *The Bodies We Were Loaned*, 2002
Hilary Tham, *Bad Names for Women*, 1989
   Counting, 2000
Barbara Louise Ungar, *Charlotte Brontë, You Ruined My Life*, 2011
Jonathan Vaile, *Blue Cowboy*, 2005
Rosemary Winslow, *Green Bodies*, 2007
Michele Wolf, *Immersion*, 2011

ABOUT THE WORD WORKS

The Word Works, a nonprofit literary organization, publishes contemporary poetry in fine editions. Since 1981, it has sponsored the Washington Prize, a $1,500 award to an American or Canadian poet. Monthly since 1999, The Word Works has presented free literary programs in the Chevy Chase, MD, Café Muse series, and each summer, free poetry programs are held at the historic Joaquin Miller Cabin in Washington, DC's Rock Creek Park. Every year, two high school students debut in the Miller Cabin Series as winners of the Jacklyn Potter Young Poets Competition.

Since 1974, Word Works programs have included: "In the Shadow of the Capitol," a symposium and archival project on the African American intellectual community in segregated Washington, DC; the Gunston Arts Center Poetry Series (Ai, Carolyn Forché, and Stanley Kunitz, among others); the Poet Editor panel discussions at The Writer's Center (John Hollander, Maurice English, Anthony Hecht, Josephine Jacobsen, and others); and Master Class workshops (Agha Shahid Ali, Thomas Lux, Marilyn Nelson).

In 2011, The Word Works will have published 73 titles, including work from such authors as Deirdra Baldwin, Christopher Bursk, Barbara Goldberg, Edward Weismiller, and Mac Wellman. Currently, The Word Works publishes books and occasional anthologies under three imprints: the Washington Prize, the Hilary Tham Capital Collection, and International Editions.

As a 501(c)3 organization, The Word Works has received awards from the National Endowment for the Arts, National Endowment for the Humanities, DC Commission on the Arts & Humanities, Witter Bynner Foundation, The Writer's Center, Bell Atlantic, Batir Foundation, the David G. Taft Foundation, and others, including many generous private patrons. The Word Works has established an archive of artistic and administrative materials in the Washington Writers' Archive housed in the George Washington University Gelman Library.

Please enclose a self-addressed, stamped envelope with all inquiries.

The Word Works
PO Box 42164
Washington, DC 20015

wordworksbooks.org
editor@wordworksbooks.org

OTHER AVAILABLE WORD WORKS BOOKS

Washington Prize Books

Nathalie F. Anderson, *Following Fred Astaire*, 1998
Michael Atkinson, *One Hundred Children Waiting for a Train*, 2001
Carrie Bennett, *biography of water*, 2004
Peter Blair, *Last Heat*, 1999
Richard Carr, *Ace*, 2008
Ann Rae Jonas, *A Diamond Is Hard But Not Tough*, 1997
Frannie Lindsay, *Mayweed*, 2009
Richard Lyons, *Fleur Carnivore*, 2005
Fred Marchant, *Tipping Point*, 1993, 3rd printing 1999
Ron Mohring, *Survivable World*, 2003
Brad Richard, *Motion Studies*, 2010
Jay Rogoff, *The Cutoff*, 1994
Prartho Sereno, *Call from Paris*, 2007
Enid Shomer, *Stalking the Florida Panther*, 1987, 2nd edition 1993
John Surowiecki, *The Hat City after Men Stopped Wearing Hats*, 2006
Miles Waggener, *Phoenix Suites*, 2002
Nancy White, *Sun, Moon, Salt*, 1992, 2nd edition 2010

International Editions

Yoko Danno & James C. Hopkins, *The Blue Door*
Moshe Dor, Barbara Goldberg, Giora Leshem, eds., *The Stones Remember*
Myong-Hee Kim, *Crow's Eye View: The Infamy of Lee Sang, Korean Poet*
Vladimir Levchev, *Black Book of the Endangered Species*

Additional Titles

Karren L. Alenier, Hilary Tham, Miles David Moore, eds.,
    Winners: A Retrospective of the Washington Prize
Jacklyn Potter, Dwaine Rieves, Gary Stein, eds.,
    Cabin Fever: Poets at Joaquin Miller's Cabin
Robert Sargent, *Aspects of a Southern Story*
    A Woman From Memphis